3279

TORNADOES

by Dale-Marie Bryan

Content Consultant
Jennifer Rivers Cole, PhD
Department of Earth & Planetary Sciences
Harvard University

CORE
LIBRARY

Published by ABDO Publishing Company, PO Box 398166, Minneapolis, MN 55439. Copyright © 2014 by Abdo Consulting Group, Inc. International copyrights reserved in all countries. No part of this book may be reproduced in any form without written permission from the publisher. The Core Library™ is a trademark and logo of ABDO Publishing Company.

Printed in the United States of America,
North Mankato, Minnesota
042013
092013

Editor: Mirella Maxwell
Series Designer: Becky Daum

Library of Congress Control Number: 2013932501

Cataloging-in-Publication Data
Bryan, Dale-Marie.
 Tornadoes / Dale-Marie Bryan.
   p. cm. -- (Earth in action)
 ISBN 978-1-61783-940-5 (lib. bdg.)
 ISBN 978-1-62403-005-5 (pbk.)
 1. Tornadoes--Juvenile literature. 2. Natural disasters--Juvenile literature. I. Title.
 551.55--dc23
                                               2013932501

Photo Credits: Rex Features/AP Images, cover, 1, 16, 45; Mike Gullett/AP Images, 4; Red Line Editorial, Inc., 7, 18; Charlie Riedel/AP Images, 8; Shutterstock Images, 10; Todd Shoemake/Shutterstock Images, 12; Powerfocusfotografie/Getty Images, 14; iStockphoto/Thinkstock, 20, 24; Getty Images/Thinkstock, 22; Orlin Wagner, File/AP Images, 26; AP Images, 28; Jim Bourdier/AP Images, 30; Sue Ogrocki/AP Images, 33, 37; Sean Steffen/The Morning Sun/AP Images, 35; T. Rob Brown/The Joplin Globe/AP Images, 38; Jim Reed/Getty Images, 40

CONTENTS

CHAPTER ONE
Tragedy in Joplin 4

CHAPTER TWO
A Tornado's Life Story 12

CHAPTER THREE
The Tornado Family 20

CHAPTER FOUR
On the Tornado's Trail 30

Ten Powerful Tornadoes .42

Stop and Think 44

Glossary. 46

Learn More. 47

Index 48

About the Author 48

TRAGEDY IN JOPLIN

On Sunday, May 22, 2011, the air was hot and sticky. As the day dragged toward evening, clouds piled higher and grew darker. Weather forecasts began breaking in on TVs in southeastern Kansas and across the state border to southwestern Missouri. The weather anchors warned of a supercell thunderstorm, which is a long-lasting thunderstorm. Supercell thunderstorms can produce the most violent

The May 22, 2011, tornado caused devastation in the city of Joplin, Missouri.

tornadoes. It was time for residents to take cover!

Touch Down

At 5:17 p.m., tornado sirens shrieked in Joplin, Missouri. The supercell thunderstorm was headed toward the city. Seventeen minutes later, the tornado touched down just outside Joplin. Within two minutes of touchdown, the tornado began tearing its destructive path through the town of 50,175 people.

The tornado's winds spun more than 200 miles per hour (322 km/h), ranking it an EF5 tornado. At some points, the tornado was nearly one mile

6

The Enhanced Fujita Scale

Scale	Wind Speed		Percentage of All Tornadoes	Potential Damage
	mph	km/h		
EF0	65–85	105–137	53.5%	Minor or no damage. Some roof or siding damage; broken tree branches
EF1	86–110	138–178	31.6%	Moderate damage. Roofs severely damaged
EF2	111–135	179–218	10.7%	Considerable damage. Roofs torn off; house foundations shifted; cars lifted off ground
EF3	136–165	219–266	3.4%	Severe damage. Entire stories of houses destroyed; severe damage to large buildings; trains overturned
EF4	166–200	267–322	0.7%	Extreme damage. Cars and other large objects thrown
EF5	more than 200	more than 322	less than 0.1%	Total destruction. Houses swept away; concrete structures critically damaged; tall buildings collapsed

The Enhanced Fujita Scale

This chart describes each ranking of tornado on the Enhanced Fujita Scale. After reading about the Joplin tornado, what advice would you include if you were making a poster about staying safe in a tornado? What information from the chart would you want to include on your poster?

The Joplin hospital was one of thousands of buildings destroyed by the EF5 tornado.

(1.6 km) wide. It moved an entire hospital four inches (10 cm) off its foundation, tore up asphalt parking lots, and tossed semitrucks and buses 200 feet (61 m). The tornado ripped Joplin High School's roof off and blew out all of its windows. Churches, grocery stores, and apartment buildings were flattened in minutes.

The tornado tore through Joplin for 32 minutes and traveled six miles (10 km). It then continued through surrounding communities for another 16 miles (26 km). It destroyed nearly 8,000 homes, businesses, schools, churches, and other structures.

It took 161 lives and injured more than 1,000 people.

One of the reasons the death toll was so high was because some Joplin citizens did not believe the tornado sirens. Missouri is part of Tornado Alley, a group of 11 states where tornadoes happen often. Joplin's tornado sirens sound off a lot. Many Joplin residents thought the sirens on May 22 were another false alarm. Even meteorologists had a hard time understanding the Joplin storm. The tornado was wrapped in rain, making it difficult to predict the speed and possible direction.

Bike Helmet Saves Boy

Not every Joplin citizen ignored the tornado sirens on May 22, 2011. Augie Ward's mother reacted quickly when she heard the sirens. Just before the Joplin tornado struck, Augie's mother told him to put on his bike helmet and get into the bathtub to stay safe. Moments later the tornado ripped out the toilet and threw it at Augie's head! His mother's quick thinking and that bike helmet saved Augie's life!

A family sorts through what is left of their home after the Joplin tornado.

Tornadoes do not only occur in Tornado Alley. They can happen elsewhere in the country. It takes certain weather conditions for tornadoes to develop. Meteorologists track storms, such as the one in Joplin, to better understand them and help prevent future loss of life. Many tornadoes have destructive effects and bring about horrible tragedies. It is important to listen to meteorologists' warnings to stay safe during a tornado.

President Barack Obama gave a speech to the Joplin High School graduating class almost a year to the day after the EF5 tornado destroyed their school and changed their lives forever:

> By now, most of you have probably relived those 32 minutes again and again. Where you were. What you saw. . . .
>
> And yet, the story of Joplin is the story of what happened the next day. . . . And all the days and weeks that followed. . . . That story is part of you now. . . . You've learned at a younger age than most that we can't always predict what life has in store for us. No matter how we might try to avoid it, life can bring heartache. Life involves struggle. Life will bring loss. But here in Joplin, you've also learned that we have the power to grow from these experiences. We can define our own lives not by what happens to us, but by how we respond.

Source: Valerie Strauss. "Obama's Joplin High School Commencement Speech." The Washington Post. May 21, 2012. Web. Accessed February 6, 2013.

What's the Big Idea?

Read the excerpt from President Obama's speech carefully. What is his main idea? What evidence is used to support his point? What things is he trying to say to the graduating class? What do you think he means when he says, "The story of Joplin is the story of what happened the next day"?

CHAPTER TWO

A TORNADO'S LIFE STORY

As the people of Joplin and the surrounding communities saw firsthand, tornadoes are one of the most violent storms in the atmosphere. Most tornadoes develop from severe thunderstorms.

Thunderstorm Formation

A thunderstorm develops from a cumulonimbus cloud. These clouds have a flat bottom and a top that looks like pieces of cauliflower. They are also dark in

Thunderstorms develop tornadoes that can quickly become violent and destructive.

A thunderstorm is fully developed when a cumulonimbus cloud gets bigger and becomes flat at the bottom.

color. As warm air from Earth rises, cumulonimbus clouds grow upward. The cauliflower-like part of the cloud gets bigger and becomes flat. When the cumulonimbus cloud looks like this, it means the thunderstorm is fully developed. This is called the mature stage.

The cumulonimbus cloud brings rain, lightning, and thunder. Hail, strong winds, and tornadoes are also possible, depending on the severity of the thunderstorm. Jet streams form the largest tornadoes on the Fujita scale. A jet stream is an area of strong winds, traveling up to 60 miles per hour (97 km/h), found in a small area of the atmosphere. Many severe thunderstorms develop when a cold front mixes with a jet stream. A cold front is the leading edge of a cold air mass, a large section of air that has similar moisture and temperature features. Cold fronts bring a decrease in temperature and humidity. If moist and dry air overlaps with a newly forming

Mr. Tornado

Tetsuya Theodore Fujita became known as Mr. Tornado. He first noticed the sharp downdrafts, currents of cold air moving downward, from a thunderstorm while on a mountaintop in Japan. Horace Byers from the University of Chicago learned about Fujita's discovery. At Byers's invitation, Fujita moved to the United States and studied airflow patterns in thunderstorms. He observed that hook echoes, fish hook-shaped patterns on radar, meant possible tornadoes. Now meteorologists knew what to look for and could give warnings in time for people to take cover. This discovery likely helped save many lives.

A supercell thunderstorm creates powerful severe weather in its path.

thunderstorm, the young storm can become a supercell thunderstorm.

A Supercell Thunderstorm

A supercell thunderstorm is the most powerful thunderstorm. It has an updraft that is constantly rotating a small current of air upward. This rotation brings warm air into the storm cloud. Supercell thunderstorms can travel for hundreds of miles and last between two and six hours. Supercell thunderstorms can create severe weather, including strong winds, large hail, and heavy rain. They can also produce the strongest tornadoes, though less than half do.

From a Supercell to a Tornado

While tornadoes do not always develop from a thunderstorm, it is possible. Tornadoes are rotating columns of air that have contact with a thunderstorm cloud and extend to Earth's surface.

What Can a Tornado Do?

There are many examples of what tornadoes have done over the years. In 1915 a canceled check from Great Bend, Kansas, was found 210 miles (338 km) away in Palmyra, Nebraska, after a tornado. A tornado lifted five train cars weighing 70 tons (64 metric tons) each off the track in Moorhead, Minnesota, in 1931. A 1953 tornado in Waco, Texas, destroyed a six-story furniture store filling the street below with bricks up to five feet (2 m) deep.

A tornado will usually develop when winds are strong and are spinning in a counterclockwise direction. Most tornadoes have winds blowing at 100 miles per hour (161 km/h) or less, but the most powerful tornadoes can have wind speeds of more than

1. Warm air rises from the ground into the bottom of the thunderstorm cloud.

2. Changing wind speeds and directions cause rising air to rotate vertically. This is called an updraft.

3. Funnel forms from the cloud base to the ground.

4. Funnel spins at tremendous speeds, picking up debris in its path.

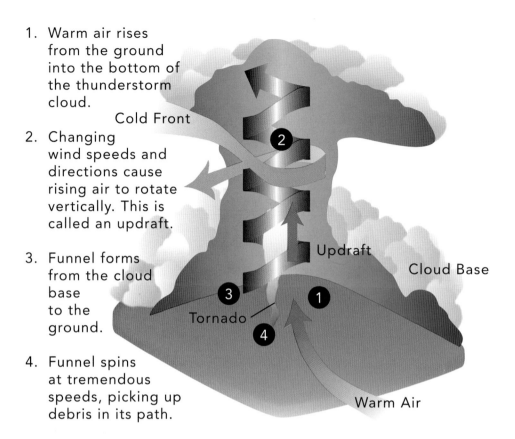

Cold Front

Updraft

Cloud Base

Tornado

Warm Air

The Anatomy of a Supercell Tornado

This diagram shows how a tornado forms from a supercell thunderstorm. Supercell thunderstorms can create the most destructive tornadoes. Based on what you have learned, what would the weather be like on a day when a supercell tornado might form?

250 miles per hour (402 km/h). The fastest tornado ever measured was 318 miles per hour (512 km/h) in 1999 in Oklahoma. Like thunderstorms, not all tornadoes are the same. A tornado can take many shapes and sizes.

This newspaper article tells of a severe thunderstorm and tornado that struck the town of New Richmond, Wisconsin, in 1899. Not only did the tornado damage much of the town, but heavy rains also washed out roads and bridges:

> Burkhardt, Wis., June 13—A messenger has reached here from New Richmond, and has telegraphed here for doctors and help, saying that the storm struck that town and a large number were killed and wounded. The railroad officials have endeavored to get out a special train, but on account of the several washouts are unable to do so, and the doctors and many others are now driving across the country as fast as horses can safely carry them.
>
> Source: "Swept to Death." The Daily Times. June 13, 1899. Web. Accessed February 6, 2013.

Consider Your Audience

Review the article closely. How could you change it for a different audience, such as your parents or friends? Write a blog post conveying this same information for the new audience. What is the best way to get your point across?

CHAPTER THREE

THE TORNADO FAMILY

People call tornadoes by many different names such as twisters and funnels. Tornadoes do not all look the same either. Scientists have different names for the way a tornado looks. Strong tornadoes in their early stages might be cone or elephant trunk tornadoes. Dying tornadoes may be called rope tornadoes for their long, thin shape. Large tornadoes with several smaller tornadoes within them are called

Tornadoes come in all shapes and sizes. Tornadoes are not limited to the United States.

Waterspouts are harder to track than a tornado on land. A waterspout is classified as a weak tornado.

multiple-vortex tornadoes. Just as there are many ways to describe tornadoes, there are several formations often confused with tornadoes.

Tornado-like Storms

Tornadoes can form or move over water. If this happens, it is called a waterspout. Waterspouts are often confused with tornadoes and are classified as weak tornadoes. A waterspout has a lower rotation than a tornado and does not extend as far into a cloud. If a waterspout spins fast enough, it sucks up water vapor. The water vapor forms into droplets, allowing the waterspout to become visible. It is hard to track waterspouts, but researchers have been able to gather some data from airplanes and ships. A few waterspouts have been tracked spinning as fast as 50 miles per hour (80 km/h). Waterspouts last between five and ten minutes.

A gustnado is another formation similar to a tornado. Gustnadoes develop above a strong thunderstorm's gusting downdraft. They last only a few minutes. Gustnadoes are shorter than tornadoes at 30 to 300 feet (9 to 91 m) high. They look wispy and are not attached to clouds. Gustnadoes can cause damage similar to an EF0 or EF1 tornado.

Global Tornadoes

Tornadoes can happen almost anywhere in the world. North America, Europe, Australia, and parts of Asia are the most heavily affected continents. The United States has more tornadoes than any other place in the

A dying tornado has a long, thin shape, similar to this tornado in Colorado.

world. These are also the most violent tornadoes.

US tornadoes are most common in an area scientists have nicknamed Tornado Alley. This area includes most of Texas, Oklahoma, Kansas, Nebraska, and Iowa. It also includes parts of eastern New Mexico and Colorado, eastern South Dakota, southern Minnesota, and western parts of Missouri and Arkansas.

Globe-Trotting Tornadoes

Tornadoes occur in other countries too. In fact, the only continent that has not had a tornado is Antarctica. Though the United States has the most tornadoes, the United Kingdom has the highest number per square mile. Canada has about 80 per year, and Japan has approximately 20 per year. Bangladesh had the highest death toll from a tornado with more than 1,300 lives lost. This may be due to the country's dense population.

Other US Tornado States

Other areas of the United States have a lot of strong tornadoes too. Wisconsin, Illinois, Indiana, and Ohio are among other Midwest states to have

Joplin, Missouri is part of the US Tornado Alley region.

tornadoes. Strong tornadoes are not limited to one or two regions. Many southeastern states experience tornadoes. These states include Louisiana, Mississippi, Alabama, Georgia, Tennessee, North Carolina, South Carolina, and Kentucky.

The Worst US Tornadoes

Tornado Alley and its surrounding states are home to the deadliest tornado of all time. This tornado affected three states —Missouri, Illinois, and Indiana— on March 18, 1925. Scientists think there may have been more than one tornado. The Tri-State Tornado lasted three and a half hours, traveled 219 miles (352 km), and took 695 lives. Murphysboro, Illinois, lost 234 citizens, the highest number of tornado deaths ever for one town.

The worst outbreak of EF5 tornadoes happened 49 years later from April 3 to 4, 1974. The storm system produced 147 tornadoes across 13 states. Tornadoes reached south to Laurel, Mississippi, north to Detroit, Michigan, and as far east as Staunton, Virginia. It took 15 hours and 2,014 miles (3,241 km)

When Do Tornadoes Happen?

Tornadoes can happen any time of the year, but they usually happen when seasons are changing. The likelihood of a tornado developing moves with the sun. In North America, early spring and late fall are the prime time for the Gulf Coast to be hit with tornadoes. Summer is the season for tornadoes along the Canadian border. And in Australia, tornadoes are most likely to occur from November to January. This is during the southern hemisphere's spring and summer.

Parts of Xenia, Ohio, were destroyed by the tornadoes that tore through the town in April 1974.

before the tornadoes stopped. Six of the tornadoes were rated as EF5s, and another 88 were rated as EF2s. Tornado, wind, and hail damage were reported in all 13 states. Xenia, Ohio, was hit the worst when one tornado traveling 318 miles per hour (512 km/h) ripped through the town.

FURTHER EVIDENCE

There is quite a bit of information about Tornado Alley in Chapter Three. It covered states included in Tornado Alley and the worst tornadoes to damage the region. If you could pick out the main point of the chapter, what would it be? What evidence was given to support the point? Visit the Web site below to learn more about Tornado Alley. Choose a quote from the Web site that relates to this chapter. Does the quote support the author's main point? Does it make a new point? Write a few sentences explaining how the quote you found relates to this chapter.

What and Where is Tornado Alley?
www.mycorelibrary.com/tornadoes

CHAPTER FOUR

ON THE TORNADO'S TRAIL

Tornadoes form quickly and are usually over in a matter of minutes. This makes them hard to study. Even though meteorologists know more about tornadoes than they used to, they still have many questions. How exactly do tornadoes form? How can we predict where tornadoes will strike? One way meteorologists learn about tornadoes is by

Tetsuya Fujita had a better understanding of tornadoes through his extensive research.

making observations and comparing notes as Tetsuya Fujita and Horace Byers did.

Another way meteorologists study tornadoes is by keeping records. They can then compare what happened in the past with what is happening now and can make better predictions for the future.

Meteorologists also model how tornadoes happen so that they can experiment and study them on a miniature scale. They may use computers to model past thunderstorms, looking for clues as to why tornadoes formed where they did. Or they may model a tornado's effects

Tornado Awareness

One of the problems with tornado warning systems today is that they warn too large an area. The sirens may go off for an entire city, when only a small section is in danger. If this happens too often, people will stop believing them. The National Weather Service is working to target their warnings better. They are also using different ways of warning people such as text messages, smartphone apps, and weather radios.

Meteorologists use computers to better understand which thunderstorms are likely to develop into tornadoes.

on a structure to discover better and stronger ways of building.

Tornado Tools

Technology developed many tools meteorologists can use to study tornadoes. One is radar. Radar was developed during World War II (1939–1945). Microwaves were beamed out, and the radio waves reflected back to an antenna. Soldiers could figure out the enemy's location, even in the dark. Since the radio waves also reflected off rain and snow, scientists realized they could use radar for detecting storms and learning more about them.

Airplanes

At the end of World War II, airplanes played a major role in helping scientists learn more about thunderstorms. Byers led a study in Florida where pilots flew planes into thunderstorms, while radars tracked the storms. This study helped meteorologists learn about the life cycles of storms.

Doppler Radar and Satellites

The Doppler radar came about around the same time Fujita devised his tornado scale. It helped him see the hook echoes of tornadoes forming supercell storms. Doppler radars could determine which way storms were moving. Computers analyzed their signals and produced images of the storms.

Doppler radar has been a helpful tool for meteorologists in predicting thunderstorm patterns.

Rockets carried satellites into space that gave meteorologists a bird's-eye view of the weather patterns and storms on Earth. The images the rockets captured allowed scientists to see weather events further in advance than they could before.

Storm Spotters and Chasers

Meteorologists needed to observe storms when and where they happened. They needed people in the middle of the action. Storm spotters are trained individuals who observe storms in their area. They report the severe weather they see. They help the weather service track storms as they happen.

Storm chasers provide in-the-field knowledge and equipment to learn even more about storms as they happen. They are trained meteorologists who often travel potentially long distances to track severe storms and tornadoes.

Storm chasers measure the humidity, wind speed, temperature, and air pressure of a storm. They also release weather balloons to capture information from within the storm. Their vehicles are equipped with Doppler radars so that they can see the storms developing on-screen, as well as outside.

Storm chasers rely on technology to help them track and measure tornadoes.

Safety First!

No matter where you are in the world, it is important to know how to stay safe from tornadoes. Even small tornadoes can pack dangerous winds and send things flying. Knowing what to do could keep you from being injured.

First of all, develop a tornado safety plan. Talk to your caregivers about what you should do if a

Joplin schools now have tornado safety shelters in case of an emergency.

tornado strikes. Know where you can go in case of a tornado. If you are inside, seek shelter in the lowest and sturdiest possible place, such as a basement. If that is not available, go to an inside room such as a bathroom, closet, or hallway, and cover yourself with blankets or a mattress.

If you are outside, go to a strong building or somewhere with a basement. If you are too far away from a building, find a low place, such as a ditch, and cover your head with your hands. Do not wait until you can see the tornado coming. Sometimes tornadoes are hard to recognize because it is too dark outside, they are too big, or they are wrapped in rain.

If you are in a car, fasten your seat belt. Tell the driver to go to a safe place, such as a nearby building. If debris starts flying, the driver should pull over. Move your head lower than the windows. Cover your head with

Tornadoes, Strange but True

- A Mississippi tornado picked up a mother and daughter in their Volkswagen and dropped them unhurt on top of an electric company building.
- A tornado in Hugo, Minnesota, stripped a tree of its leaves but neatly replaced them with pieces of pink insulation.
- Oklahoma City, Oklahoma, holds the record for having the most tornadoes in the past 90 years. They've had 90 tornadoes!
- Tornadoes struck Codell, Kansas, on May 20 in 1916, 1917, and 1918.

Meteorologists and storm chasers are working hard to understand thunderstorms and tornadoes so they can better predict them in the future.

your hands, a blanket, or a coat. If possible, get out of the car and find a low place to take cover.

If you are at school, follow your teachers' instructions. Stay out of big rooms like the gym. Crouch beside a sturdy, interior wall, sit elbows to knees, and cover the back of your head with your hands.

Tornadoes and the Future

No matter how much information scientists collect about the weather, they can't change it. They are worried people's actions may be causing the patterns to change. Some scientists believe global warming may cause more severe weather and stronger tornadoes. But scientists are working hard to learn how to predict them better. They are also studying storms and damage of the past to learn how to build stronger and safer structures. The best thing we can do is to learn all we can about how to keep ourselves safe when tornadoes strike.

EXPLORE ONLINE

One focus of Chapter Four is tornado safety. In thunderstorms there are other things to watch out for. The Web site below has safety tips for different types of weather. As you know, every source is different. How do the tornado tips on the Web site compare with what you learned in this chapter? What are other things to remember for staying safe in a thunderstorm?

Tornado Safety
www.mycorelibrary.com/tornadoes

TEN POWERFUL TORNADOES

May 7, 1840
Natchez, Mississippi: Estimated EF5
The Great Natchez Tornado tracked along the Mississippi River, first touching down in the port city of Natchez. It tore the city apart, and destroyed many flatboats. The Great Natchez Tornado accounted for 317 deaths in Louisiana and Mississippi.

May 27, 1896
Saint Louis, Missouri: EF4
At least 255 people were killed when an EF4 tornado swept through Saint Louis. The actual death toll was likely much higher, since officials did not count the number of people killed who were living in shanty boats on the river.

March 18, 1925
Missouri, Illinois, and Indiana: EF2-EF5
The Tri-State Tornado took 695 lives, the highest number recorded in the United States. This tornado traveled 219 miles (352 km) for more than 3 hours.

April 6, 1936
Gainesville, Georgia: EF4
Two tornadoes merged over Gainesville on the morning of April 6. The tornadoes left four city blocks of damage, killing more than 200 people and injuring 1,600 people.

April 9, 1947
Woodward, Oklahoma: EF5
The Woodward tornado destroyed more than 100 city blocks in its path. More than 180 people died.

May 9, 1953

Waco, Texas: EF5

Known as the deadliest tornado on record in Texas, this tornado tore through downtown Waco destroying more than 1,000 businesses and homes. Approximately 2,000 cars were also destroyed or damaged. More than 114 lives were lost.

June 9, 1953

Massachusetts: EF4

The tornado in 1953 is the worst tornado on record in New England. It spawned from a thunderstorm that began in Kansas on June 7. This tornado traveled 46 miles (74 km) in 84 minutes, destroying or damaging 4,000 buildings in its path. Ninety-four lives were lost, and more than 1,000 people were injured.

April 3–4, 1974

The Midwest, Southeast, and Northeast regions: EF4 and EF5

During a 24-hour period, 147 tornadoes broke out, causing damage in 13 states and killing 315 people. The storms spawned 30 EF4 and EF5 tornadoes.

April 25–28, 2011

The Southeast and Northeast regions: EF4 and EF5

On these record-setting days, more than 358 tornadoes were produced from a single storm. In total, 328 lives were lost from the largest tornado outbreak.

May 22, 2011

Joplin, Missouri: EF5

The Joplin tornado was the deadliest since modern record keeping began in 1950. There were 161 lives lost that day.

Why Do I Care?

This book discusses how tornadoes have affected many people's lives. Even if you have never experienced a tornado yourself, how do the victims' experiences connect to your life? Maybe you have experienced another weather-related disaster. Write down two or three ways a tornado victim's experiences connect to your life.

Dig Deeper

What questions do you still have about tornadoes? Do you want to learn more about the anatomy of a tornado? Or storm chasing? Write down one or two questions that can guide you in doing research. With an adult's help, find a few reliable new sources about tornadoes that can help answer your question. Write a few sentences about how you did your research and what you learned from it.

Surprise Me

Learning about tornadoes can be interesting and surprising. Think about what you learned from this book. Can you name two or three facts in this book that you found most surprising? Write a short paragraph about each. Describe what you found surprising and why.

Tell the Tale

Chapter One discusses the Joplin, Missouri, tornado. Write 200 words that tell the true story of this event. Be sure to set the scene, develop a sequence of events, and offer a conclusion.

GLOSSARY

cold front
an advancing edge of a cold air mass

debris
materials picked up in or caused by a tornado

downdraft
a current of cold air that moves downward

gustnado
a short-lived vortex that forms in front of a storm-related gust front

hook echo
radar patterns observed during a thunderstorm, appearing like a fish hook

meteorologist
a scientist who specializes in things that happen in the atmosphere

supercell storm
a long-lasting thunderstorm that causes severe weather and tornadoes

Tornado Alley
an area of the United States where tornadoes often occur

updraft
a current of air that moves upward

vortex
a mass of swirling water or air

waterspout
a vortex that spins rapidly and extends beneath a cloud over water

LEARN MORE

Books

Bechtel, Stefan. *Tornado Hunter: Getting Inside the Most Violent Storms on Earth*. Washington DC: National Geographic Society, 2009.

Carson, Mary Kay. *Inside Tornadoes*. New York: Sterling, 2010.

Gibbons, Gail. *Tornadoes*. New York: Holiday House, 2009.

Web Links

To learn more about tornadoes, visit ABDO Publishing Company online at **www.abdopublishing.com**. Web sites about tornadoes are featured on our Book Links page. These links are routinely monitored and updated to provide the most current information available.

Visit **www.mycorelibrary.com** for free additional tools for teachers and students.

INDEX

airplanes, 22, 34
Australia, 25, 27

Bangladesh, 25
Byers, Horace, 15, 32, 34

Canada, 25
cloud base, 18
cold front, 15
cumulonimbus clouds, 13–14

Doppler radar, 34, 36
downdrafts, 15, 23

Fujita Scale, 6–7, 15
Fujita, Tetsuya Theodore, 6, 15, 32, 34

gustnado, 23

hook echoes, 15, 34

Japan, 15, 25
jet stream, 15
Joplin, Missouri, 5–11, 13

mature stage, 14
mesocyclone, 18
meteorologists, 9–10, 15, 31–32, 33, 34–35, 36
multiple-vortex tornadoes, 23

National Weather Service, 32
New Richmond, Wisconsin, 19

Obama, Barack, 11

rope tornadoes, 23

storm chasers, 36
storm spotters, 36
supercell thunderstorm, 5–6, 16, 18, 34

thunderstorms, 5, 13–16, 18–19, 23, 32, 34, 41
Tornado Alley, 9, 10, 25, 27, 29
tornado safety, 37–41
Tri-State Tornado, 27

United Kingdom, 25
updrafts, 16, 18

Ward, Augie, 9
water vapor, 22
waterspouts, 22–23

Xenia, Ohio, 29

ABOUT THE AUTHOR

Dale-Marie Bryan writes for children at her Kansas country home in the middle of Tornado Alley, 40 miles from Joplin, Missouri. She has seen two funnels in her life but hopes she never has to see a tornado up close.